MARKET SKETCHBOOK

25th Anniversary Edition

UNIVERSITY OF WASHINGTON PRESS   **Seattle and London**

MARKET
SKETCHBOOK

By Victor Steinbrueck

This new edition of *Market Sketchbook*, with contributions by Peter Steinbrueck and Marjorie Nelson Steinbrueck, is published with the support of the Friends of the Market on their twenty-fifth anniversary.

Copyright © 1968, 1978, 1996 by the University of Washington Press
Third printing, 25th Anniversary Edition, 1996
Printed in the United States of America

Library of Congress Catalog Card Number 68–8513
ISBN 0–295–97556–3

The paper used in this publication meets the minimum requirements of American National Standard for Information Sciences—Permanence of Paper for Printed Library Materials, ANSI Z39.48-1984. ∞

Foreword

In the first edition of *Market Sketchbook* in 1968, my father Victor Steinbrueck wrote, "Seattle's Pike Place Market deserves more than a book. It deserves to live on, as a link with Seattle's past, a meaningful and much loved part of its present, and a place of unlimited possibilities for its future." Thankfully, it was decided by a vote of Seattle's citizens that the market did indeed deserve to live on. This special edition of *Market Sketchbook* commemorates passage of the 1971 citizens' Market Initiative which saved the market from the urban renewal wrecking ball twenty-five years ago. The Market Initiative was sponsored by the Friends of the Market and was the culmination of eight years of dogged determination and uncompromising dedication to protecting and defending the market's existence from those who would destroy it.

Since its inception, Seattle's much-loved Pike Place Market has weathered more than one battle for survival. The farmer's market was officially established in 1907 to protect both farmer and consumer from the self-serving efforts of wholesale houses and middlemen who sought to raise produce prices and profit off local farmers. In the 1960s, it was urban renewal, backed by downtown poohbahs and redevelopment interests, that threatened the continued existence of the market. The initiative put a decisive end to that bleak episode and opened the door for federal urban renewal funds to be spent, for the first time, on restoration and rehabilitation rather than on removal of so-called urban blight.

Then in the late 1980s, as the renovation of the market neared completion and the market's future appeared bright and secure, the unthinkable happened. A group of private real estate investors from New York, known as the Urban Group Investors, claimed that they had purchased the *public* market through a series of complex tax syndication agreements with the nonprofit Pike Development Authority (PDA). They threatened to drastically raise rents and do away with marginal businesses if their demands for higher profits were not met. A group of irate citizens and market merchants quickly formed the Citizens Alliance to Keep the Pike Place Market Public to combat the investors. After a protracted, multifront legal battle involving the Citizens Alliance, the City of Seattle, the PDA, and the Urban Group, the market was finally extricated from the Urban Group's grip. Ironically, it was the preservation ordinance passed by the Market Initiative that served to invalidate the Urban Group's legal claim to ownership of the market.

As an ordinance, the concept of historic preservation embodied in the original Market Initiative was perhaps the broadest and most inclusive ever enacted in the United States. Not only did the ordinance create the Pike Place Market Historic District for the architectural preservation of core market buildings, but it also called for the ongoing preservation of the historic, cultural, social, and economic qualities that characterized Seattle's central farmer's marketplace. This form of historic preservation was untried before, but was deemed necessary if the purposes of the initiative, of truly saving the market, were to be fulfilled.

Twenty-five years should be enough time to measure the initiative's success. Were the preservation goals fully achieved? As I remember the market before the initiative, it was in some respects a different place from what it is today. There were fewer tourists then and more "two bag" shoppers, toting home groceries and fresh produce. A large community of mostly low-income residents surrounded the market, but shoppers came regularly from far and wide to take advantage of abundant local, fresh farm produce and hard-to-find ethnic foods and groceries. Mom-and-pop businesses proliferated, as did secondhand stores and inexpensive goods outlets. In winter, however, the main arcade in the market appeared partially empty at times, as there were fewer vendors to fill the day-stalls during the farmers' off-season. The market buildings were crusty and decrepit-looking, with facades obscured by a clutter of excessive signage and layered paint. Many buildings were in fact in serious decay.

Today, the market from all appearances is thriving. The old buildings have been handsomely renovated and new buildings sensitively integrated. Farmer presence is up, and there is a bustle of activity throughout the year, with street performers adding a festive atmosphere. To be sure, the sights, sounds, and smells of the market are much the same as they've always been. And no one doubts now that saving the market was one of the best things that ever happened to Seattle.

What has changed is some of the clientele, and the market's shopping orientation with it. As hordes of tourists throng to see the famed market, businesses cater more to the souvenir-seekers and to travelers' appetites, farmers sell more processed and packaged goods that are easier to ship and less bulk produce and fresh vegetables. Traffic and parking can be a miserable experience for local residents trying to make their way to the market from other parts of the city, grocery shoppers find it harder to squeeze through to the farmers' stalls on summer weekends, and the supporting downtown resident population has shrunk.

The question is, can the market survive, as local residents have long known and valued it, in a changing world where the "Meet the Producer" concept of the shopper-who-buys-a-bag-of-carrots-from-the-farmer-who-grew-them-down-the-road is an anachronism? If the quality and character of the market are to be truly preserved, the market must remain true to its historical functions and avoid self-parody. Farmers, merchants, and vendors must resist the pressures to cater to the tourist clientele, and not let the local shopper become alienated and squeezed out. Most importantly, the market must continue to provide an abundance of fresh, local farm produce, specialty foods, and goods of real quality that will continue to attract local shoppers.

Seattle deserves such a place.

PETER STEINBRUECK
June 1996

Tribute to Victor Steinbrueck and the Market Initiative Victory

Victor Steinbrueck's awareness of and appreciation for the unique character and history of Seattle as well as the natural beauty of its surroundings were reflected in a charming colored-pencil drawing that he sketched when he was six years old. It was of a single, gently drifting sailboat on Puget Sound with the city and the Olympic Mountains in the background. At age six Victor titled his drawing "I See a City."

Throughout his life Victor looked at his environment with the eye of an artist, the spirit of a philosopher, and the critical judgment of an environmentally sensitive architect and civic planner. His love affair with Seattle was lifelong. Through his writings, books, art, and architecture—including the design of three parks—he was a staunch and indefatigible activist for all that he considered best for Seattle and its people. He often said, "I'm just trying to do the right thing." I smile to think that if Victor had been proclaimed king of Seattle, "it would have indeed been a wonderful and miraculous reign."

As a professor of architecture and urban planning at the University of Washington for more than thirty years, Victor passed on to his students his sense of integrity and dedication to the ideals and philosophy of the humanist. Over the years his dreams and hard work were many times blocked by city politics, bureaucracy, and a value system in which opportunism, greed, and the rampant bulldozer held sway. Fortunately, however, there has been enough enlightened civic leadership in Seattle's history that Victor's voice was heard, and his recommendations were followed in two major areas: Pioneer Square and the Pike Place Farmer's Market.

More than twenty-five years ago, Victor was asked by the Seattle City Council to provide a historic survey of Pioneer Square. Because of his architectural knowledge of the area and his sensitivity to the need for buildings to relate to one another and to their blocks, we enjoy there today a viable and colorful neighborhood. He put that same knowledge into his many years of dedicated work as president of the Friends of the Market, resulting in the market initiative victory of 1971. The "Friends" saved not just one or two renovated buildings but an entire community. The initiative won a seven-acre historic district and set up an historic commission to oversee additions and changes.

In 1996, despite much paved-over farmland and market stalls overflowing with crafts and T-shirts, the small farmers' produce stands still shine and the market thrives as a wonderful panoply of life, color, sound, smells, and entertainment. Yet, it is in danger of losing its character, of becoming a commercialized and cheaper version of a farmer's market. Victor Steinbrueck would say that it is to everyone's advantage that it remain a true farmer's market—not only for Seattle residents but for tourists to enjoy as well.

Victor wrote in 1981 in an article commemorating the market initiative: "My feeling is and always has been that the victory for the people of Seattle in keeping the market through a popular vote is a tribute to the people themselves. It could not have happened without the participation of everyone involved and to them should go the thanks, not to any one person."

MARJORIE NELSON STEINBRUECK
June 1996

PIKE PLACE MARKET INITIATIVE

INSTRUCTIONS TO SOLICITORS

1. Voters must be registered in City of Seattle.
2. Voters should sign EXACTLY AS REGISTERED. (If the voter is registered as John B. Smith, he should sign that way and NOT J. B. Smith or other form of name).
3. Voters should fill in all spaces where possible.
4. Voters may sign Initiative Petition only once. (If voter signs more than once, the signature is lost completely, and voter is subject to legal penalty).
5. Use either pen or pencil, however pen is preferable.
6. Every name counts so return every petition no matter how few names.
7. Payment for circulating petition is prohibited by law.
8. Return all petitions to:

FRIENDS OF THE MARKET
91 Pike St., Seattle 98101

Shall the City of Seattle preserve, improve, and restore the Pike Place Markets by creating a Pike Place Market Historical District and providing for administration and enforcement?

INITIATIVE PETITION BY THE VOTERS OF SEATTLE TO THE HONORABLE CITY COUNCIL OF THE CITY OF SEATTLE, WASHINGTON:

We, the undersigned citizens of the State of Washington and qualified electors of the City of Seattle, do hereby respectfully petition you that the proposed ordinance, a full, true and correct copy of which is on the opposite side of this petition, be enacted by the Council, or submitted to the voters of the City of Seattle, and each of us says: I have personally signed this petition; I am a qualified and legal voter of the City of Seattle and my address is correctly stated opposite my name.

No __1702

	PETITIONER'S SIGNATURE (Signature Mandatory)	PRINT NAME	ADDRESS IN SEATTLE	PRECINCT (If Known)
1.				
2.				
3.				
4.				
5.				

WHO OPPOSES THE INITIATIVE?

Downtown business interests and Urban Renewal investors have hired a large advertising agency to defeat the initiative. While some owners and merchants have joined their campaign - the effort is financed primarily by people who hope to profit from Urban Renewal.

WHO SUPPORTS THE INITIATIVE?
MARKET MERCHANTS:

Angus McDonald	Brehm's Delicatessen
Marjorie Randall	Queen Anna Antiques
Art Bauder	"Art's Antiques"
Mondo Martinez	Vegetable Vendor
Herbert Chilcote	Dexter Gallery
H.W. Foster	J.W. Dunn Seed Co.
Jack Levy	City Fish Co.
Gary Levy	City Fish Co.
Melvin Wertz	Queen Anna Gifts
Zenda Sawyers	Zenda Gifts
Gary W. Lee	Dexter Galleries
June Leslie Ray	Victrola Tavern
Cory Hiporx	Hideout Tavern
M.J. Thomas (Julian)	Swanberg's Gifts
Lloyd Graves	Alaska Trade Building
Nita Carlson	The Art Stall
Frank Miller	Soup & Salad
Mrs. Ruby Peters	Three Girls Bakery
Charles Brenner	Three Girls Bakery
William Burke	Sasquach
Jean Stafford	Manticore
Tom Westlake	Sasquach
Albert H. Haru	A.H. Fruit
Margaret Minaglia	Farmer
Cipriano L. Primero	Farmer
John Foster	J.W. Dunn & Co.
Mary E. Skruber	St. Vincent de Paul
Alyce Knight	St. Vincent de Paul
Helen Rossman	St. Vincent de Paul
Laurence J. Howard	Larry's Barber Shop
Jeanne Rath	Deluxe Delicatessen
Orion Rath	Deluxe Delicatessen
Mrs. Helen Yokoyama	Roy's Market
Richard M. Yokoyama	Roy's Market
Ruby Rutelonis	Spice Shop
Ada Wilson	Barber Shop, Ada's
Pat Forrester	Brass Bell
Jerry Dominago	Farmer
Tony d'Pietro	Farmer
Rufino Ordonio	Farmer
Tina Ordonio	Farmer
Andy Padua	Farmer
Mildred Padua	Farmer
Alex Malina	Farmer
Sabina Malina	Farmer
Tomas Viloria	Farmer
Mary Viloria	Farmer
Charles Hanoh	Pike Place Fish
Roy Yokoyama	Roy's Fruit
Joan Ford	B & B Donut
Pasqualina Verdi	Farmer
Gregg Rechtin	Manticore
Dorette English	Manticore
Margurite Mann	Mug's Antiques
Rich Mann	Mug's Antiques
Winnie Buchong	Elsie's Barber Shop
Mary Cantil	Elsie's Barber Shop
M.J. Bighu	Admiralty Antiques
Beth McCormick	Aunty Beth
Peggy Randall	Deluxe Bar-B-Que
Janis Gesinger	Market Space #31 Antiques
Mary Medalia	Herb Seller
Mureleen Benton	Rabbit Farm
Alex Tadique	Elisa & Eleana
Tony Genzale	Farmer
Tony Marrese	Arcade #8
Maurice B. Randall	Deluxe Bar-B-Que
Lulu Bell Parker	Deluxe Bar-B-Que
Christine J. Allen	Deluxe Bar-B-Que
John Yokoyama	Pike Place Fish
E.R. Brown	Pike Place Fish
R.O. Cromwell	Athenian Cafe
Tulane Holmes	Athenian Cafe
Katherine Kea	Athenian Cafe
Chris Ebowlet	Athenian Cafe
Lenamae E. Huggin	Athenian Cafe
Odalor E. Giub	Athenian Cafe
Madeleine Malino	Athenian Cafe
Viktor Korozijo	Dry Vendor

The Alliance for A Living Market
Supports the Market Initiative

SEATTLE CITY COUNCIL CANDIDATES

Bruce Chapman	John Miller
James Kimbrough	Bill Harrington
Tim Hill	Sam Smith
	Jodi McCracken

If you want to help Friends of the Market, call MA 2-2595.

Pike Place Market Initiative
VOTE NOVEMBER 2, 1971

VOTE YES
"LET'S KEEP THE MARKET"

"The market is a fragile kaleidoscope of merchants, mostly foreign born and fiercely independent. It provides an income for dozens of small businessmen and women of a breed embodying all the virtues, now almost gone, that we believe made America great." Elizabeth Tanner

FRIENDS of the MARKET
Victor Steinbrueck, PRES.

Introduction: 1978

Ten years after this book was first published, the Pike Place Market is still alive, still the most colorful peopleplace in Seattle, but experiencing drastic urban renewal "improvements." After numerous prolonged City Council hearings and a lengthy but successful citizen initiative and election campaign, to fulfill the Friends of the Market slogan, "Let's Keep the Market," remains the first priority—but open to various interpretations. Now protected as both a local and a national historic district, the market nevertheless remains vulnerable to inappropriate modification. While its physical survival has been assured, there remains the danger that the commonplace nature of traditional uses and structures may not be successfully retained. Ironically, those in charge of keeping the market—the bureaucrats, the developers, and the architects—are now to be feared.

The historic basis of the market is the selling of local produce and other food as well as serving the needs of low- and middle-income shoppers by small, owner-operated businesses. The market environment consists of unpretentious, small-scale structures, constantly remodeled and modified to adapt to changing needs. Now these anonymous, unglamorous structures are in the process of being extensively "rehabilitated" to comply with urban renewal requirements according to plans by the public development authority and its architects. Contemporary design and entrepreneurial judgments are establishing a new, more luxurious market character, sometimes tinged with a "plastic" quality as some of the natural awkwardness of the old environment is removed. Most of the remaining original structures in the historic district—the Sanitary Market; the Stewart House; and the buildings housing the Council Thrift Shop, Rogers Clothing, the Seattle Garden Center, and the Rendezvous Tavern—have been slated for demolition and replacement. Some will survive because the Friends of the Market and other market friends have been insisting on enforcement of urban renewal plans which give first priority to rehabilitation.

One of the enduring joys of market shopping is the presence of local farmers and their marvelously attractive fresh produce. Some of the elder farmers shown in this book are no longer alive or have given up selling here, but the total number slowly increases as new young farmers come in, many of them encouraged by county and federal economic assistance for the purchase of development rights to protect existing local farmlands. Other new farmers have learned the potential of selling in the market, and several are being financed by the market development authority. At the same time, there has been an increased public awareness of the satisfaction to be gained from buying fresh produce from the farmers themselves. The farmers are the leading attraction in the market; if they ever leave, the market will truly be dead.

Many of today's market people are not those portrayed in this book. Gone are most of the low-income, single-room-occupancy residents who established the human basis of the area. Their numbers have dwindled from 700 in 1968 to 90 a few years ago. Subsidies have so far provided remodeled or new quarters for 170, with 350 units required at the completion of urban renewal. Gone or transformed are many of the modest, low-income-oriented shops, cafes, and taverns. Some simply took their urban renewal relocation or going-out-of-business money and went away. Others have been upgraded to an unmarketlike and inappropriate poshness that mocks the intention of the preservation ordinance and the historic commission.

Food merchants still predominate along the main market arcade and across Pike Place, although, as with the farmers, some of the oldtimers shown in this book are gone. Like everything else, such businesses have had an upward economic trend, now tending to serve middle-class patrons with gourmet tastes rather than filling low-income needs. There is only one butcher selling cheap meats, and soft fruits and vegetables are no longer offered as these proprietors have sold out to others who have upgraded their businesses. Still remaining and thriving are some of the old standby merchants—Don and Joe's Meats; Pike Place Fish (Yokoyamas); Pure Food Fish (Amons); City Fish (Levys); Manzo's, Collelo's, and Constantino's fruits and vegetables; and others. Junk and odd-lot stores are giving way to antique dealers and crafts merchants, and there are many more stalls selling imports and souvenirs. Anyone can become a merchant for the two-dollar price of a day stall.

New shops selling imported foods and tourist items are also changing the market's personality, though sometimes in a colorful way. Although market preservation guidelines do not allow chain enterprises or shops catering only to tourists, enforcement of such requirements is difficult. It has become a serious problem to keep the market primarily for the people of this area, as has been its traditional nature. If this can be achieved, it will also retain its unique attraction for visitors. An additional concern for the future is whether the people's market that was voted for in 1971 can survive the changes of drastic urban renewal, involving either the rehabilitation of familiar buildings or their replacement with new and larger structures. Nearby developments also threaten, including more than three hundred middle-income and luxury condominiums to the north which represent an obvious trend away from the old market life style. The legal act of establishing a protective ordi-nance for the market was a tremendous people's victory, but the real achievement of that goal is proving to be even more difficult.

Introduction: 1968

When I was growing up in Seattle, shopping trips to the Pike Place farmers' market were a regular part of our family activities. During the twenties and the thirties the market was large and prosperous, and I naively assumed that a farmer's market was an essential part of every city, like a post office and a railroad station. I remember my first trip to Los Angeles in 1935, when I looked forward to seeing the highly publicized produce of sunny California, but found nothing comparable to our Pike Place Market. Since those days, an artificially created farmers' market has appeared in Los Angeles, offering a horrible example of what could happen in Seattle.

My attachment to the Seattle market has led me to look for interesting markets in other cities and countries wherever I have traveled. I have found the markets not only a source of fresh local produce and inexpensive goods, but places of great regional color, surely one of the best means of getting acquainted with a locality and its people. Historically they have usually been located at the center of the town, often next to the town hall. A fascinating study could be made of the markets of the world, and like many people I believe the Pike Place Market of Seattle would rank among the most unusual and colorful.

This sketchbook is intended as both a visual exposition of the Pike Place Market area and a personal statement concerning the unique urban and architectural qualities found there. As an architect, as well as a citizen who uses and enjoys the market, I am interested in the physical aspects of the place and in the people and their activities. The actual buildings themselves—the forms and flow of space within these humble structures—provide a rich esthetic experience which is meaningful to everyone and of particular interest to architects and artists. Part of the subtle charm of the market area is the intrigue of exploration and the element of surprise as one moves through the various streets, lanes, passageways, ramps, and stairs. The plan of the main market building shows seven stories, with areas at the lowest level labeled, among others, "chicken shop," "apple storage," and "room with water under floor." Details like the columns with ornate capitals, and the rows of naked light bulbs that give the arcades a festival air, add to the visual delight of the market and offer lessons to architects who look beyond their books.

The market offers an urban educational experience in the broadest sense by enabling people, and especially children, to see facets of humanity, activities, and aspects of the city not easily accessible elsewhere. Because there is no better place to shop for the best fresh produce, for out-of-the-ordinary foods, and for inexpensive goods of all kinds, the market is a prime shopping area for low-income people—its primary reason for existence—and for gourmets of every economic level. Nowhere else is there to be found such a broad social mixture going about its business in a natural and uninhibited way. People of all races, all religions, all nationalities, and all income levels come together freely to work and shop, to linger and look and enjoy themselves in an atmosphere traditionally and necessarily free of prejudice. Here is the dramatic experience of people acting out their daily existence through face-to-face encounter and involvement, in contrast to the sterile, dehumanizing environment that has grown to be typical of much of our urban world.

Through sixty years of growth and change, the market has developed its unique character and special quality, prospering in good times and surviving through difficult days. Now the market and the district around it are facing obliteration or drastic, "urban renewal," as serious consideration is being given to proposals that will eliminate most of the buildings, remove the residents of the area, and radically modify the environmental setting of market life. First Avenue would be seriously disrupted. Foremost among those who defend the market as a vital part of the city and the region are the Friends of the Market, a volunteer civic organization formed in 1963 under the wing of Allied Arts of Seattle and "dedicated to saving and renewing the historical Pike Place Market and district through a program of community planning." These are people who recognize the importance of urban continuity, and who see in the market area the kind of environment where the new can be allowed to grow up alongside the old, without destroying it; where a variety of forms and functions can be accommodated, to the inestimable enrichment of the city and its people.

Seattle's Pike Place Market deserves more than a book. It deserves to live on, as a link with Seattle's past, a meaningful and much-loved part of its present, and a place of unlimited possibilities for its future.

Seattle needs the market.

VICTOR STEINBRUECK

Seen from under the rusty marquee of the Sanitary Market building, Pike Street widens into a sort of plaza to accommodate the street ramp up from the lower Post Street to the south, and probably originally to make room for the horse and wagon vendors. By a rather considerable stretch of imagination this space could be called Pike Plaza, but this title is much too impressive to be associated with the traditional Pike Place Public Market. A few years ago there was a metal pergola at the center walk, but it was too much trouble for the city to maintain it. The simple large red sign with the clock is an identifying landmark visible all the way up Pike Street and in reverse from Elliott Bay and the nearby waterfront. Always a busy scene of shoppers and trucks, the world of the market begins here for most people.

Looking north up Pike Place from the office of Richard Desimone, in the Bartell Building, the market activity is partially surveyed. Richard Desimone is president of the Pike Place Public Markets, Inc., and one of the sons of Joe Desimone, the Italian immigrant who was owner of the market for many years. In view are the Leland Hotel, a portion of the public market, the so-called Sanitary Market, and First Avenue. The activity visible here is a good barometer of the day's business in the market. This is where the market began on a hillside road in about 1906.

Along First Avenue the next street to the north is Pine Street, which drops suddenly to Pike Place and the market. Elliott Bay and the islands of Puget Sound come into view in the vista between U-Save Drugs and Roger's Army and Navy Store. The market announces itself with another red-lettered sign thrust high above its roof and visible from far up Pine Street.

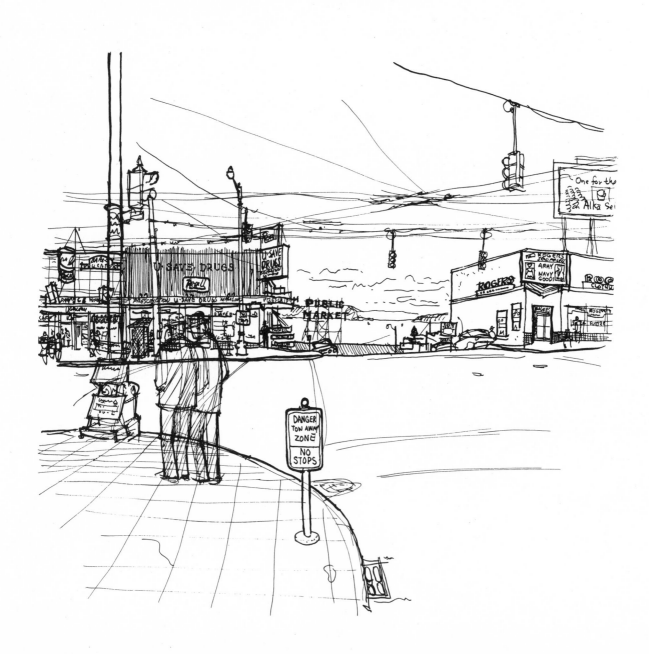

As we move westward down Pine Street below First
Avenue, the brick-lined alley to the south affords an
approach to the lower shops of the Sanitary Market
as well as a glimpse of busy Pike Place with the Farmers'
Market and the LaSalle Hotel beyond.

Half a block farther down, Pine Street meets diagonal Pike Place with its continual vehicular traffic not only of shoppers but of service trucks on both sides of the street. To the west is Pike Place Public Market, which can be entered here at the location of the City Fish Company. On the east are other market shops with such offerings as fresh ripe fruits, meats (formerly including horse meat), sausages, bakery goods, poultry and eggs, salvage clothing and surplus goods, and a few small cafés.

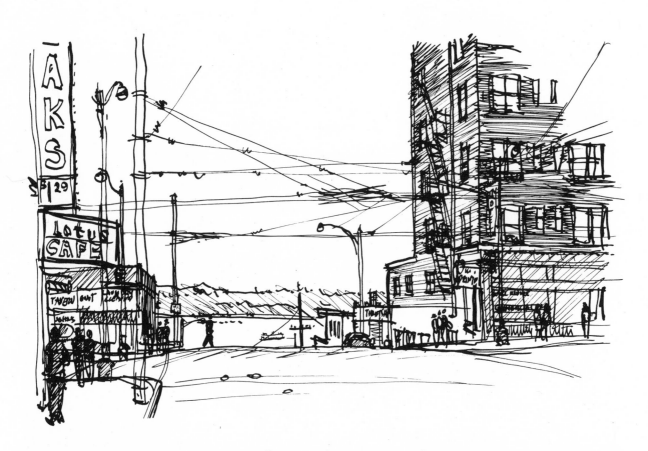

As we continue up First Avenue to the north, the next cross street is Stewart Street. First Avenue twists here toward the northwest. This is the highest elevation of the area. Again, there is an open vista to Elliott Bay. The farmers' market becomes a single narrow low roof under which the market parking area is approached. In former years this parking space was another wing of the market, but it was destroyed by fire several years ago. On both sides of Stewart Street are some of the many shops that are part of the market environment and support it as a great low-income shopping area. Salvage clothing and surplus stores, taverns, small hotels, and rooming houses are an integral part of the ecology of the market.

ST. VINCENT DE PAUL maintains a salvage clothing and rummage store fronting on both Stewart and Pine streets. There are nine such salvage shops related to the market. All are apparently thriving, and they form an essential part of the attraction of the market. Prices are very low, and occasional finds in antiques or junk items spur on the curious.

Looking south on Pike Place from the foot of Stewart Street offers a continuing panorama of busy traffic supervised for many years by the cordial policeman Percy, who first worked here as a mounted officer. Part of the intriguing quality of the market is its variety of approaches and exits.

GILL BROS. SEATTLE GARDEN CENTER sells the largest variety of seeds in the Northwest. It has been in this same location since World War II. Most of its business is with people who come from outside the area by car or bus. In the distance is the Bartell Building, housing Mr. Desimone's office.

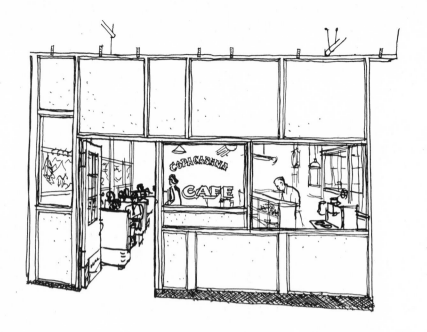

Past the open-air stalls of Pike Place and deep into the Sanitary Market building is the small COPACABANA CAFE presided over by genial Ramón Palaez, former Bolivian journalist. Sometimes other members of his family assist. The simple menu in Spanish lists no more than half a dozen items, all delicious. The most famous dish, sopa de camarones, a highly spiced shrimp soup, is a meal in itself. The Copacabana radiates an atmosphere of warmth and friendliness. Often customers drop in to practice their Spanish with Mr. Palaez.

The tiny THREE GIRLS BAKERY has been here since 1920 with Nicolai and Vera Kusminski as the working proprietors since 1957. The shop is a sales outlet for Brenner Brothers bread. It sells 100 per cent rye bread and 55 other varieties, including Logan bread for skiers and hikers and flat bread. Like many other market people, the Kusminskis have an interesting background. Mrs. Kusminski, who was born in Vladivostok, was a midwife in Germany and has delivered over two thousand babies!

Under an ancient metal sidewalk marquee on the east side of Pike Place are more open-air markets offering unusually low-priced produce and foods. Here are Gabrielle's Fruits and Vegetables, South Park Poultry and Eggs, Irene's Snack Bar (featuring Swedish pancakes), Cut Rate Fruits, Cut Rate Meats, John Yellam Vegetables, Viking Cheese, Three Girls Bakery, Russell's Meat Market, and Almeleh's Fruits and Vegetables. In the open Sanitary Market Building are Milwaukee Sausage, Crystal Meats, Philadelphia Fish Market, Surplus Groceries, the Copacabana Café, and other shops. For years the Horse Meat Market was also in this location.

Upstairs is the studio home of the talented and successful artist Richard C. Hickson, who is too little known locally. His second-floor row of window boxes is always filled with flowers. For him, the market provides a congenial and anonymous home and constant inspiration.

Farther along First Avenue at
Lenora Street many older buildings,
built during the last decade of the
nineteenth century at the time
of the Alaskan Gold Rush, come
into view. Picturesque but
neglected remnants, these fine
examples of past styles have
become the subject of controversy
as to their value and use. Sympathetic
restoration potentials of such
buildings are obvious for those who
have eyes to see, and have proved
economically feasible elsewhere.
The salvation of these precious
and irreplaceable elements of
the area's heritage, which lend
spice to the city scene, depends
on the whims of politicians and
their chosen architects.

Viewed southward from Virginia Street, First Avenue presents a solid block of substantial architecture from the heydays of the city's past, providing a consistently interesting backdrop for Seattle's most dramatic and colorful street. Continued use of these pleasant buildings, with creative restoration when necessary, will contribute to both the historical perspective and the architectural variety of the central business district.

There are many streets, but there is only one First Avenue, Seattle, Washington, U.S.A. It is a honky-tonk street harking back to Seattle's early booming years of shipping and lumbering. Instead of being slicked up or wiped out entirely, this street should be encouraged to go on the way it is. Here is a slice of life, frank and honest, with the dramatic experience of its daily existence. To deny it is to deny life.

"THE PIKE PLACE MARKET. It reveals the face of truth. Its roughness reminds me of Seattle's beginnings, its lusty past, the vitality that gave it national notice long ago.

"It is an honest place in a phony time. While the advertising, public-relations syndrome gains, the market is a haven where real values survive, where directness can be experienced; where young people who have never known anything other than precut meat, frozen vegetables, or homogenized milk can discover some things that they do not see on television or in Disney picture books or movies. They will discover that milk is really made up of two parts—skim and cream; that tenderloin steaks are the least part of a steer, and that carrots are more green than orange. They will learn that food can be preserved even without freezing machines; that such native preserving methods as smoking and kippering or salting bear the additional gift of the heightened flavor. They will also find out that most people are not well dressed, and others are not clean. This will do them good.

"The Pike Place Market is worth holding on to because it is unique in our area. And yet it does need help. It needs the hammer and paintbrush, not the black ball of destruction. It also needs the revitalizing influence of new customers, people who live nearby and will not add to the automobile traffic jam. There are many magnificent sites along the hill with spectacular views of the harbor just waiting for a sensitive entrepreneur. This is about all the market does need—some loving care and new housing nearby, together with better parking facilities. It will then survive with its own fine character.

"Let us keep this market that each generation may discover it in turn."

—Fred Bassetti, Seattle architect

Looking south down First Avenue from the corner of Pike Street presents a scene of continuous day and night activity induced by the nature and variety of the many establishments located here. In this single block, on both sides of the street, are a drug store, a clothes store, an all-night motion picture theater, a fresh doughnut shop, one of the most complete hardware stores in Seattle, a pet shop, a passport photographer, amusement arcades, a peep show, a cabaret, a pawn shop, an antique shop, a barber shop, a shoe shine stand, several cafés, several hotels, several taverns, and a tattoo artist. On a clear day, Mount Rainier can be seen in the distance.

South from Pike Street on First Avenue, bustling
establishments serve low-income and working-class
clientele day and night. No longer the prosperous heart
of Seattle, or the rough roaring street of a busy waterfront
town which it once was and still vividly recalls, First
Avenue retains a special character derived from its
involvement with a certain aspect of Seattle life. Its
continuity as the city's most unusual pedestrian street
from the Skid Road to Bell Town gives color and
identity to Seattle.

Most of the city's pawn shops
are strung along First Avenue.
They are intriguing places for
browsing, offering unusual items
and bargains while serving an
economic need for many. There
are many specialty stores here
along with the taverns and
cheap hotels, supplying sporting
goods, hardware, radio and
electrical goods, surplus supplies,
leather goods, pets, and clothing.
First Avenue has many taverns
and small restaurants which serve
as the working man's Rainier and
Harbor clubs.

The attraction of First Avenue is partly its uniqueness and partly that it reveals a slice of true life and character out of the past-and present-of this lumbering and shipping town. The street's constant activity demonstrates that it fills a need in the lives of many people. The urban educational experience of learning about other kinds of people is here.

In the market area there are many hotels occupied by semipermanent tenants, although transients are also accommodated. While there are some poorly maintained places, many are surprisingly clean and well kept according to low-income standards. These hotels often provide minimal housekeeping facilities, and their residents are an essential part of the market's economic base as well as its personality and character.

An aerial view of the Pike Place area helps in visualizing the relationship of the Pike Place Public Market to its immediately supporting environment of small shops, taverns, hotels, and parking areas. The relation and proximity to the central business district to the east (lower left) is shown. The Alaskan Way viaduct and Elliott Bay waterfront piers appear beyond (above). Some streets and buildings have been identified to assist orientation and comprehension.

The vital relationship of this most interesting area to downtown Seattle is apparent. It gives much-needed life and interest to what has been called a rather bland urban core.

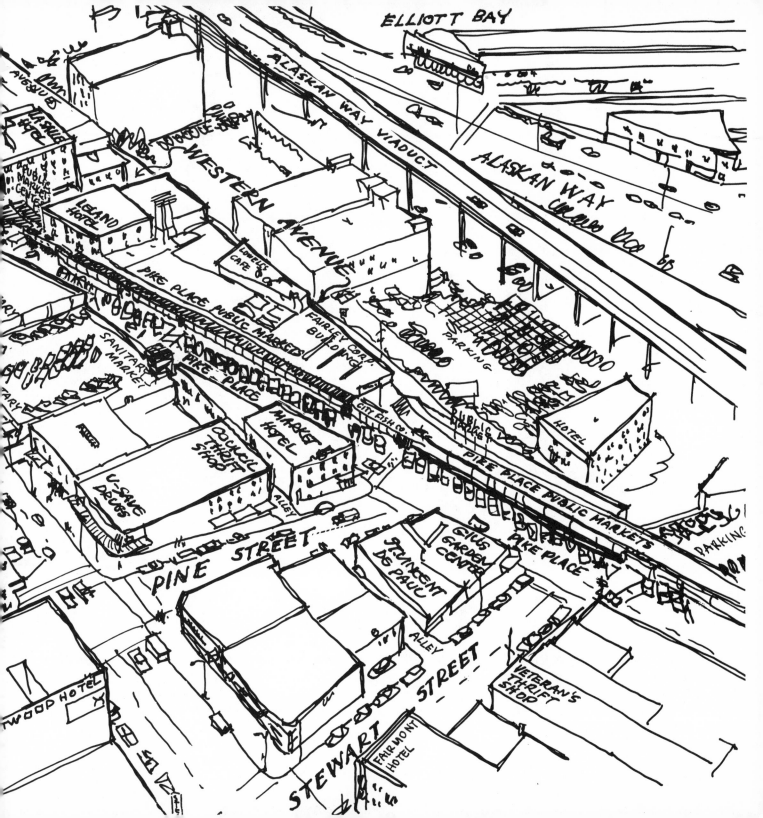

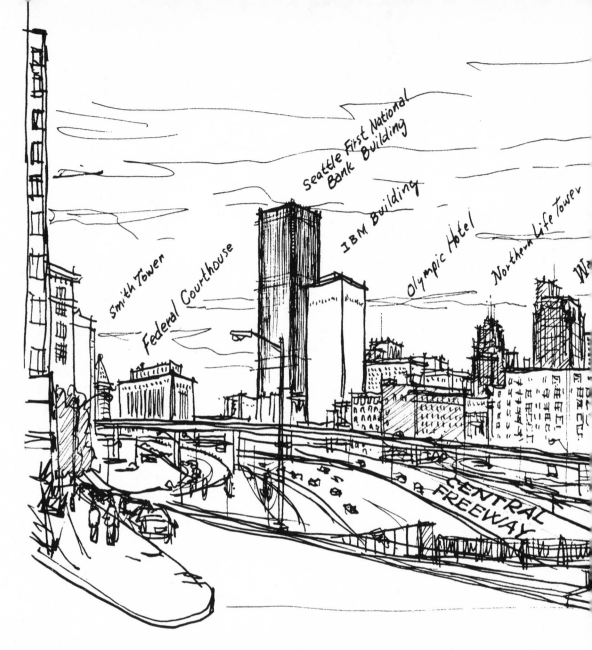

Smith Tower

Federal Courthouse

Seattle First National
Bank Building

IBM Building

Olympic Hotel

Northern Life Tower

CENTRAL FREEWAY

An almost classic approach to the Public Market is from the east down Pike Street. This broad view from above Terry Avenue across the open visual outrage of Seattle's Central Freeway reveals many of the central business district's key buildings which are identified in the sketch. The Pike Place Public Market's red-lettered PUBLIC MARKET CENTER sign and clock are noticeable even from this distance.

As we proceed westward toward the market, the character of Pike Street changes with each successive avenue intersection, culminating at First Avenue in the market's arcade past the Drug Mart Drugs. Woolworth's and Kress's ten-cent stores at Third Avenue and Penney's largest department store at Second Avenue obviously have both a geographic and economic relation to the market. The red-lettered PUBLIC MARKET CENTER sign and clock, like the market itself, are city landmarks helping to pull Pike Street shoppers and tourists down to the city's most colorful location.

At First Avenue and Pike Street, the character of the market begins to be revealed. It is a hustling, bustling scene of essential human activity. The life of the city flows through here. It is not a lonesome place.

The Bartell Building is on the left with the Leland Hotel and the Farmers' Market beyond. To the right is the Sanitary Market Building, and up First Avenue looms the multistoried Terminal Sales Building.

In the brightly lit arcade on the left are Jess Brown's DRUG MART DRUGS, Moss Kaijioka's WONDER FREEZE, Pinkey Almeleh's FRUITS and VEGETABLES, the QUAD-A ARTS stall, the NATIONAL BANK of COMMERCE (Pike Place Branch), the FRIENDS of the MARKET office, Maurie Randall's DELUXE CHICKEN BAR-B-Q CAFE, and Yazamon Nomaguchi's BEST FLOWERS with DAN'S MEATS beyond. To the right are some of the city-administered farmers' stalls where long-time market vendors Maria Iannicello, Amondo Martinez, Eddie Minaglia, Tom and Mary Viloria, and others sell their produce. The Vilorias are Alaskans and were written up in the local press recently for the achievement of raising peanuts on their farm near Kent. The revelations of the market experience begin for those who have eyes to see and ears to hear as well as noses to smell. There is no admission charge for this dramatic urban theater in the large, and you are part of it,

The ART STALL is run by twelve women artists who are members of Quad-A Arts Club, which has approximately fifty members. For four years they have conducted a successful operation in the market, and they have become one of its features, offering a variety of original artwork including prints, drawings, watercolors, and oil paintings.

Above the farmers' stalls are lovely ornate Victorian cast-iron column capitals amidst the dazzle of rows of incandescent light bulbs. People ask, "Why don't modern architects do things like that?"

Maurie's DELUXE CHICKEN BAR-B-Q CAFE is operated by friendly, smiling Maurie and Peggy Randall. Maurie is retired from the Air Force. Their specialties are delicious barbecued chicken and ribs as well as fried chicken. They have a large take-out trade, and their shop is one of the places where market people like to meet over a cup of coffee to swap gossip and trade stories.

The NATIONAL BANK of COMMERCE, one of the trustees of the Joe Desimone estate (which owns much of the market), opened this Pike Place Branch several years ago. Decorated in neo-Victorian manner, this small bank is one of the recent pleasures of the market. It is valuable and significant to have such an important institution sympathetically committed to the public market.

"Of cabbages and kings." The fresh vegetables and fruits of the Puget Sound region are unsurpassed in the world. Here they are still sold by the farmers who raise them, as they were when the market was founded for this very purpose sixty years ago. The loss of rich farmlands to industry and housing is a severe problem not only for the market but for the amenities and welfare of this region. In the prime farmlands of the Green River Valley, Boeing Aircraft has now become king.

BEST FLOWERS has been operated by Yazamon Nomaguchi and his wife for the past thirteen years although they have been Seattle florists for almost forty years. Mr. Nomaguchi is an expert in traditional Japanese dancing, which he still continues to perform.

As we proceed toward the end of the entrance arcade, space opens up to the right of Dan's Meats as the floor also ramps downward.

DAN'S MEATS is owned by Dan Sandall, grandson of the original owner, Dan Zido, and thus the third generation of marketeers. Dan's has been in the same location since 1923 and in the market for half a century. Available here are suckling pigs, tripe, sweetbreads, brains, beef bacon, and fresh ham along with all the usual meat items and special cuts or styles of meats. Dan's also does a great deal of wholesale business with some of the finest restaurants.

To the left of Dan's Meats stands the PIKE PLACE GROCERY, a cavernous space with labyrinths formed by high piles of cans and cartons. The owners are Mr. and Mrs. Fred Eisler, who have been in the market for twenty-four years. The arrangement of the merchandise is random - that is, all paper products are not necessarily in the same location, and various sized packages of the same product may be aisles apart. Shopping here is an adventure.

Another kind of open concourse space reveals itself framed by Pike Place Fish and Roy's Fruits and Vegetables on the west, with a narrow daylighted opening to the bay beyond inviting observation. Farther to the north is the main arcaded lane of the market. To the east is the broad opening to the street.

PIKE PLACE FISH is owned by Johnny Yokoyama, son of the owners of the adjacent produce stand. The fish market handles forty-five varieties of fresh seafood in season, including squid and octopus all year. Carlos Hanoh, the friendly Greek linguist, works here, serving customers of many nationalities and often conversing with them in their native tongue—French, Spanish, Italian, Hebrew, Greek, Polish, German, Japanese, or English.

ROY'S FRUITS AND VEGETABLES takes its name from its owner, Roy Yokoyama, who with his wife, Helen, has been in the market for twenty-eight years. Their children help, too. The displays are appetizing, colorful, and enhanced by the paper-bag signs which Mr. Yokoyama paints with a Japanese ink brush. Their fruits and vegetables are always fresh and good.

Beyond, to the right, stairs and ramps beckon to the lower spaces.

A glimpse of Elliott Bay lures the stroller onto a balcony which is also the approach to the La Salle Hotel and the Place Pigalle Tavern. On a clear day the grandeur of Puget Sound explodes upon the observer.

Back in the concourse in front of Roy's Fruit and Vegetable Stand another broad opening to the east is exposed. Traffic and pedestrians from Pike Place and the Sanitary Market approach here and reluctantly share the space with the constantly arriving and departing delivery trucks.

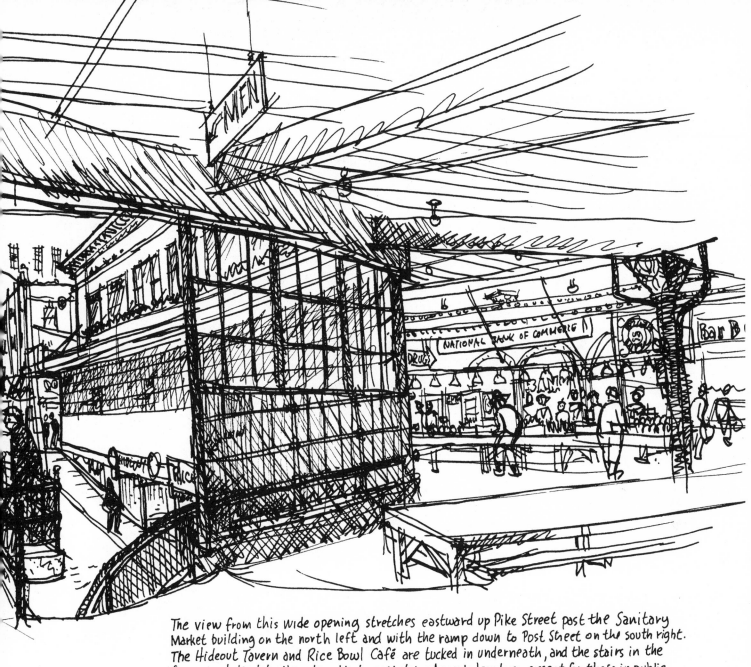

The view from this wide opening stretches eastward up Pike Street past the Sanitary Market building on the north left and with the ramp down to Post Street on the south right. The Hideout Tavern and Rice Bowl Café are tucked in underneath, and the stairs in the foreground lead to the only publicly maintained men's lavatory - except for those in public buildings - in the central business district. Pike Street's axial relationship to the market is apparent from here, and the character of downtown Seattle is exposed.

This sketch by Mark Tobey is one of many of his works inspired through the years by the people and the environment of the market. Tobey's market studies have contributed significantly to his fame as one of the world's greatest living artists. He is completely devoted to the retention of the market as an area of singular human value for the city. Many artists continue to find the market a timeless place of intense and varied esthetic and dramatic experience.

The sketch was published in "The World of the Market" by Mark Tobey (University of Washington Press, 1964), and the following quote is from the book's Introduction.

"The sketches in this book show my feeling for the Seattle Market perhaps much better than anything I can say about it. And yet there seems to be a need to speak, today, when drastic changes are going on all around us. Our homes are in the path of freeways; old landmarks, many of a rare beauty, are sacrificed to the urge to get somewhere in a hurry; and when it is all over Progress reigns, queen of the hollow streets shadowed by monumental towers left behind by giants to whom the intimacy of living is of no importance. The moon is still far away, but there are forces close by which are ready, with high-sounding words, to dump you out of bed and tear from your sight the colors of joy. And now this unique Market is in danger of being modernized like so much processed cheese.
"The Market will always be within me. Established back in 1907 by the farmers themselves—not for the tourist trade, but as a protest against the high prices paid to the commission men—it has been for me a refuge, an oasis, a most human growth, the heart and soul of Seattle.
"In the twenties, after many years in New York, I walked down this fabulous array of colors and forms. So many things are offered for sale—plants to be replanted; ropes of all kinds; antiques; Norwegian pancakes made by an old sea captain, to be eaten on one of the four stools on the sidewalk looking in. I hear the calls to buy—'Hey, you, come over here for the best tomatoes in the Market.' Across the street are open shops under long burnt-orange-colored awnings.
"The L-shaped Market is alive with all kinds of people, from everywhere, dressed in all kinds of garments, walking under the long shed studded on either side with little cafés, restaurants, and stalls. One man could be from the Black Forest in Germany, and the woman just passing the cucumber stall walks with the stateliness of an Italian princess. Among the men darting here and there is one unsteady on his feet, just dodging the green posts placed at intervals.
"Gathered in small groups like islands in the constant stream of people are the men for whom the Market is more than a place of gathering, almost a home. They live in furnished rooms and rundown hotels, some of them habitués of Skid Road at night and the Market in the day. From the many faces I picked out one man as someone I would like to know. He had looked at me with his friendly eyes—I felt he knew me, so why not speak? 'What is your lineage?' But I did not expect the answer I got. 'Adam and Eve, just like you, my son.'
"I ran into my friend again. It was summer, and he was wearing a tropical helmet topped with a small carved wooden duck. His long, yellow-white hair was piled inside. His beard, starting around his eyes, flowed down almost to his waistline. 'Come to my studio and let me paint you,' I said. 'You are an artist, why don't you paint your impression?' I made no further comment. He was a king of the Market.
"For me every day in the Market was a fiesta. But, alas, wars came; the old men I had learned to know died; more and more stalls were empty; the Japanese were sent away. Mrs. Morgan, who ran a flower stand, said, 'Mr. Tobey, the market ist deadt!' The years dissolve, and I return to visit the Market. A few old friends remain—the brothers of the fish stall, but the interesting sign above their heads has been stolen. The chairs that ascended the incline directly below them, upon which tired shoppers used to rest, have been torn out. But the main part of the Market is still active, still varied, exciting, and terribly important in the welter of overindustrialization. There is the same magic as night approaches: the sounds fade; there is an extra rustle everywhere; prices drop; the garbage pickers come bending and sorting; the cars leave the street which reflects the dying sun. The windows are all that remain of light as the sun sets over the Olympics. A few isolated figures appear and disappear, and then the Market is quiet, awaiting another day."

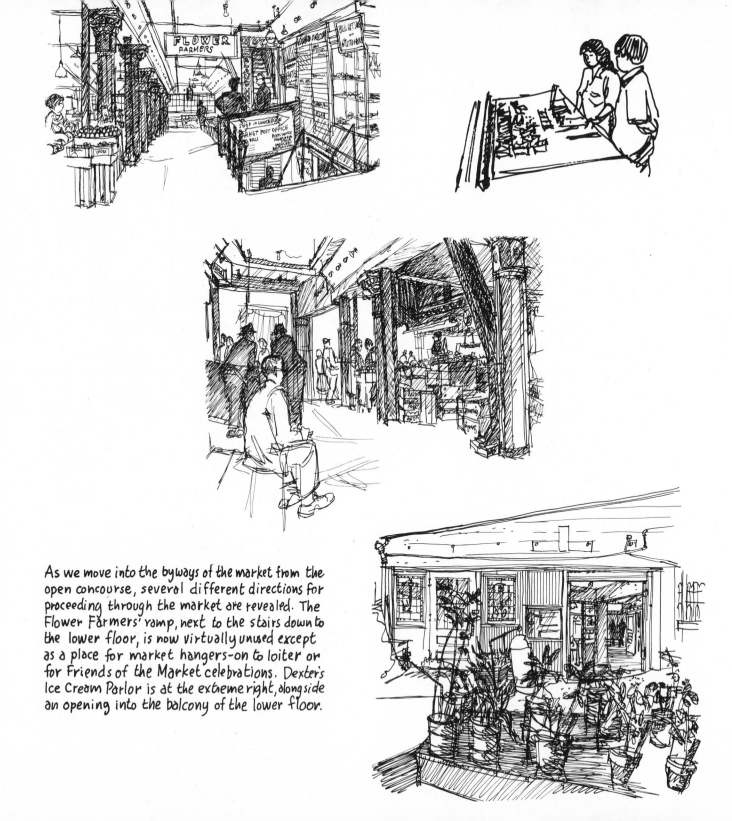

As we move into the byways of the market from the open concourse, several different directions for proceeding through the market are revealed. The Flower Farmers' ramp, next to the stairs down to the lower floor, is now virtually unused except as a place for market hangers-on to loiter or for Friends of the Market celebrations. Dexter's Ice Cream Parlor is at the extreme right, alongside an opening into the balcony of the lower floor.

The ROTARY GROCERY, operated by Raleigh and Kate Taylor since 1949, has been in business at that location since the market began. The Rotary Bakery was begun by Raleigh's father in 1919. The grocery was acquired later, and now the Bakery is operated by others. Large and varied stocks and fair prices are their specialties along with friendly helpfulness. They are among the market's mainstays.

As we proceed into the long lane of the market paralleling Pike Place, the local farmers' stalls are on the right with an enticing series of food shops and other attractions opposite. The farmers come mainly from the Duwamish or Green River valleys.

The long main arcaded lane of the market continues on for several hundred feet. Just beyond the Rotary Grocery is BREHM'S DELICATESSEN, now owned by Angus McDonald. It has been in continuous operation since about 1910, beginning as the original 'home of Brehm's famous pickles and delicatessen products. Available at very reasonable prices are twenty-seven varieties of domestic and imported cheeses, sandwich meats and sausages of all kinds, freshly made bulk peanut butter, and pure horseradish, made without fillers. Only the most Spartan can pass by without purchasing something.

A row of columns capped with ornate plaster and sheet metal capitals tends to separate the pedestrian traffic. The open colorful vegetable stalls are dramatized by the green hooded floodlights which are characteristic of the market. In the past the farmers were mostly Italian and Japanese immigrants, and there are still many Italians here. The shameful World War II evacuation completely wiped out the Japanese farmers. Now there are many Philippine farmers as well as a large number identifiable only as just plain Americans. Usually C. Primero, Rufino Ordinio, Andy Padua, and Jerry Domingo, assisted by various members of their families, sell their squash, pumpkins, cabbage, greens, and other vegetables in this location. Tony Di Pietro is an Italian farmer who has been selling here for half a century. The produce is brought in from the farms early in the morning, and the stalls are vacated every evening for washing down.

An inviting slot to the left reveals itself as yet another rampway to the lower floor, indicated by the large directional arrow sign overhead. The ramp leads directly to the "market master's" office. Here the City Health Department maintains its administration and supervision of the local farmers' portion of the market according to a system which has become traditional to the farmers, who rent stalls on a daily basis for eighty-five cents with water or fifty cents for a dry stall. It is not generally known that the city does not own any of the market but leases the farmers' locations from the Pike Place Public Market corporation on an annual basis for a token consideration.

On the opposite side, a service opening and exit to Pike Place also affords access to car parking and to the Sanitary Market building across the street. This daylighted opening gives visual and spatial relief to the continuous row of stalls, counters, and regular windows.

As we continue on, the bright, clean, large open space of the Pure Food Markets, selling meats, delicatessen, and fish, come into view. Opposite are the stands of Quality Fruits and Vegetables, a small doughnut café, and a Philippine import shop, contrasting with the open local produce counters on either side. Beyond there is a visual closing up of the space.

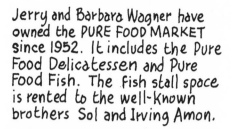

Jerry and Barbara Wagner have owned the PURE FOOD MARKET since 1952. It includes the Pure Food Delicatessen and Pure Food Fish. The fish stall space is rented to the well-known brothers Sol and Irving Amon.

Jerry Wagner has been a butcher in the market area since World War II. The meat market sells only highest grade meat of all kinds, often specially cut. The Wagners take pride in keeping their stall clean and sparkling and have a large clientele of regular customers. For a long time they featured their own sausage, made right in the market by a German specialist.

B AND G DONUTS is now owned by "Jo" (Geraldine) Felkey, since her husband, Roy, died early in 1968. Plain doughnuts and holes are prepared here each morning, adding a wonderful aroma to this section of the market. Light snacks and coffee are served along with a good view of the market crowds.

QUALITY FRUITS AND VEGETABLES (Arcade No. 8) is the stall where the handsome young man keeps up a carnival spiel in a loud singsong while you order— "I got two lettuce, one cucumber, one bunch of bananas!" He snaps bags with élan, joshes all the ladies, and has a smile for everyone. This is "Bo" Colello, whose uncle, Tony Morese, has been coming to the market for fifty years. Bo's father, Bill Colello, sold on farmers' row, and Bo helped in the summertime and on Saturdays.

In front of the Athenian Lunch and Tavern, the lane narrows considerably because the front partitions of the Athenian and of Lowell's Café are brought forward contrasting with the open shops on either side. Across the arcade, the small Philippine Import Shop and another closed fruit stall beyond reinforce the visual tightening of the space of the lane.

On the left is PURE FOOD FISH operated by Sol and Irving Amon, who contribute their share of flavor to the market, both with their colorful personalities and with their attractive displays of fresh seafoods. Dungeness crabs are always featured along with other Northwest specialties. Sol Amon, the tall one, has a spiel for passers-by as well as customers, including his appreciative "Hubba-hubba" when an interesting girl walks by.

THE ATHENIAN LUNCH AND TAVERN offers good
inexpensive breakfasts and lunches, as well as
the largest variety of beers to be found in the
city. Fifteen foreign beers are listed in addition
to many American brands. The long bar is always
filled with chattering customers. A few booths
at the windows take advantage of the
panoramic harbor view.

LOWELL'S CAFE has three floors and a most impressive view of Puget Sound and the Olympic Mountains to the west. Manning's Restaurants originated in this location in about 1908, moving on to become an extensive chain of restaurants and bakeries along the entire Pacific Coast. Manning's sold out to another owner who ran the cafeteria for six months, and then Reid Lowell acquired it in 1957. Excellent coffee and a cafeteria with hot food keep the tables filled from morning till late afternoon. The market regulars gather for a cup of coffee and a chat in the midmorning and midafternoon. The Desimones can usually be found here at coffee break times along with butchers, fish men, and farmers. Mr. Lowell would like to have a liquor bar and has been encouraged to do so, but the ambiguity of the market's future has restrained him from making the additional investment.

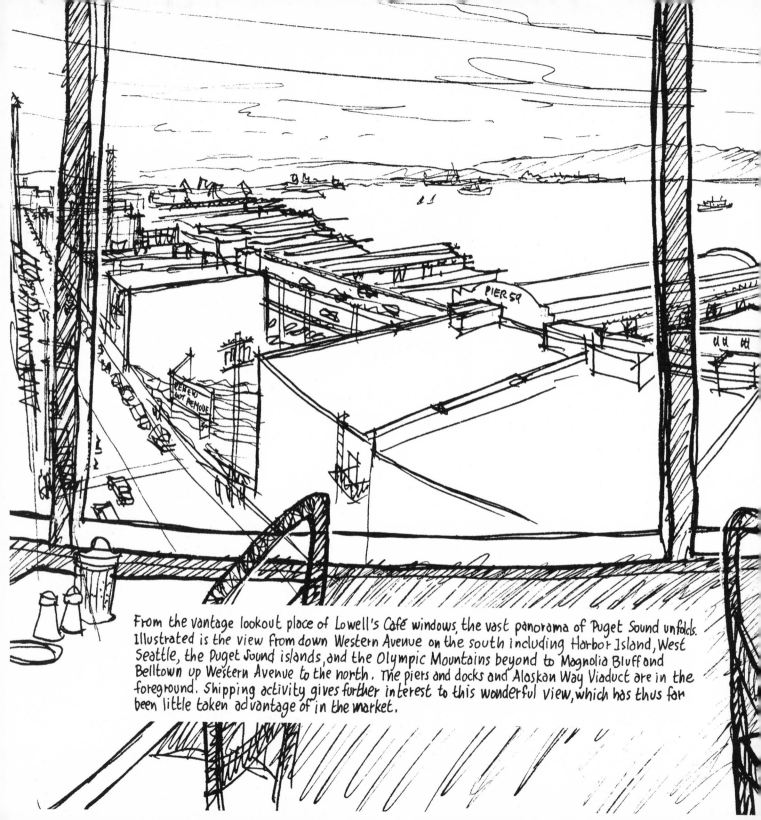

From the vantage lookout place of Lowell's Café windows, the vast panorama of Puget Sound unfolds. Illustrated is the view from down Western Avenue on the south including Harbor Island, West Seattle, the Puget Sound islands, and the Olympic Mountains beyond to Magnolia Bluff and Belltown up Western Avenue to the north. The piers and docks and Alaskan Way Viaduct are in the foreground. Shipping activity gives further interest to this wonderful view, which has thus far been little taken advantage of in the market.

This section of the market is owned by the Fairley Corporation, Morris B. Hanan, president. Mr. Hanan has operated fruit and vegetable stands in Seattle for half a century, but he is now retired from this work and manages his properties from his office off the stairs to Western Avenue.

At this spot, the Mossafers have been selling fruit since 1914. They are Sephardic Jews, one of the groups that has kept the market going since the beginning. There are no better fruits or more courtesy and friendliness available anywhere than offered here. The first fruits of the season are always available, and often special items are flown in from California, Arizona, or Hawaii.

NICE
SOLID

2
FOR
29¢

SWEET
INDIAN
PINK

5
FOR
48¢

HOME
GROWN
BEAN

29¢
POUND

SWEET
PEACHES

2
POUNDS
29¢

Since World War I there has been a meat market in this location of LOBACK'S MEATS.
Dave Loback bought there in 1946. When he died in 1952, his widow, Lois Loback, now Mrs.
Austin, carried on their business. Ed Perry, the shop manager, has been there since
1946, too, as has Margaret Olson, who works at the counter. She is a friend of the
Lobacks who came in the beginning "just to help out."
Mrs. Austin also owns Russell's Market in the Sanitary Market Building across Pike
Place. She says Mr. Loback always had faith in the market and at one time owned five
meat markets in the area. All beef is utility grade, with pork and other meats of higher
grade, so the prices are low and the shop is popular with economy-minded customers.

Another section of farmers' stalls opposite the Mossafers and Loback's has been passed on the right. In all their fresh delight, these vegetables are an irresistible visual and gustatory attraction. University of Washington Press editor, Naomi Pascal, wrote of "the gleaming ranks of tomatoes, radishes, and scallions... a kind of apotheosis of the vegetable." in referring to Mark Tobey's translation of these things into his art.

The necessities of the farmer-vendor's trade are scattered about, along with the cast-away trimmings of the produce on display — well-used boxes, tubs of water, knives, brushes, brown paper bags, newspapers for wrapping, improvised cash boxes, and scales. Framed and brightened to a glistening sparkle by the hooded overhead floodlights, these displays of local produce are an important part of the charm of the market and of the pageant of the Puget Sound country.

All farmers are welcome to sell their produce although there are formalities that must be followed, since in the beginning there was serious concern that the market should offer only genuine local produce raised and sold by the farmers themselves. They are "protected" by city ordinance, and the market stalls are managed by a "market master," Marvin Reed, in the employ of the City Health Department. After paying a three-dollar annual fee and certifying that he is a bona fide farmer, the farmer may rent a stall with water for eighty-five

cents a day, or without water for fifty cents. The farmers go to Reed's office on the lower floor at about eight o'clock every morning to pay this fee and to draw for their location for the day. The unloading and setting-up operation then commences, and selling goes on until about six in the evening or earlier if the farmer sells out his load. Boxes are packed up, and the market stalls are left to be cleaned out and washed. Refuse is left to be hauled away by the city.

There has never been any promotional program to inform farmers about the market
or to invite them to use it. Now farmers from other locations besides the traditional
ones are beginning to realize that the market offers opportunities to them, too.
Some modernization of management and promotion would probably benefit the
market.

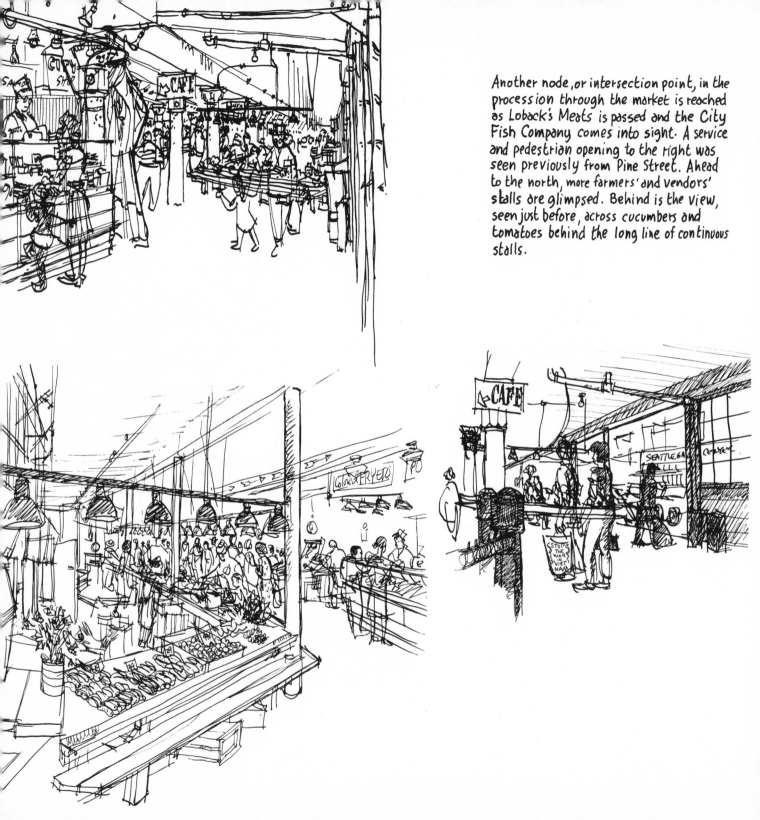

Another node, or intersection point, in the procession through the market is reached as Loback's Meats is passed and the City Fish Company comes into sight. A service and pedestrian opening to the right was seen previously from Pine Street. Ahead to the north, more farmers' and vendors' stalls are glimpsed. Behind is the view, seen just before, across cucumbers and tomatoes behind the long line of continuous stalls.

The CITY FISH COMPANY offers quality fresh seafoods. This is another small family business typical of the market. The Levy family has owned and operated it since 1922, with brothers Jack and Gary continuing on after their immigrant father, David Levy, died in 1947. Whatever seafoods are in season are available at their clean stall. They ship crab and salmon, guaranteed to arrive in good condition, anywhere in the United States. Their business, like that of many other market merchants, is an intimate, personal, sincerely friendly relation with their customers. You know that they like people.

As we look back from in front of City Fish, the steep ramp to the lower floor attracts us with the appeal of the unknown space beyond and the large directory of merchants and services there.

Beyond this juncture, another lane open to the street continues on to visual infinity with farmers vending their produce from city-leased stalls on the right. Small individual merchant vendors of all sorts sell from stalls on the left rented from the Pike Place Public Markets Corporation. Italian-born Joe Parente sells fresh eggs and garlic as well as vegetables. Mrs. Barbara Wilke sells rabbits raised at her Wilderness Rabbit Farm. Art Bauder is the big handsome fellow who offers campaign and slogan buttons of all kinds. Live earthworms and "organic" plant soil are available from George Hewett's stall. Various other miscellaneous articles are offered from day to day by other vendors. Almost anyone can arrange to sell here by contacting Mr. Desimone of the Pike Place Public Markets Corporation.

The ceiling with its electric light bulbs and the ornate columns are outstanding features of this passageway, which also affords an approach from the north on Western Avenue past the site of the old historic State Armory, carelessly destroyed by the city early in 1968.

As we move down the matted ramp toward the lower floor, a pause to look back up reveals the daylighted space which has been a turning point in the market exploration. A narrow opening to the east, or left as one proceeds down the ramp, is a stair exit to Western Avenue past the office of Morris B. Hanan, president of the Fairley Corporation which owns this section of the market building.

ELISA AND ELENA'S CAFÉ is owned and operated by Philippine-born Alex Tadique. There are only ten stools in this small place with the large view overlooking Elliott Bay. Mr. Tadique cooks authentic Philippine specialties.

The passageway ramp to the lower floor has several shops, one of which is ADMIRALTY HOUSE ANTIQUES, owned and operated by three school teachers, Fred Dau, Bill Haegele, and Don Voris. In their stock are excellent Northwest items, and such things as old bottles, furniture, and ephemera at reasonable prices.

BOOKS AND RECORDS CELLAR has been here for seven years although the owner, Ron Layton, had been in the book business for ten years before. He specializes in foreign records and out-of-print book items. Used comic books can be had at rock-bottom prices. Browsing is invited.

Homemade soup, hot casseroles, chili beans, and other home-cooked foods at reasonable prices ("pay when served") are offered by the RED WING CAFÉ. The colorful decor is a visible record of changing times and different owners over a period of years. The pink and blue phase, the bright red and white era, and the green kitchen with the new linoleum period are mementos of past efforts to decorate and dress up the place over a period of years. The present owners are new to the market and are trying hard to build up a regular clientele.

Norwegian-born Mrs. Anna Myklebust has run MYKLEBUST'S OLD TIME SHOP since 1930. Miscellaneous antiques are offered. Mrs. Myklebust remembers the Goodwin Brothers, who built and then rebuilt most of the market in its present form. She also recalls when the market area included many wooden houses. Her market hours are irregular now because her health has "not been so good lately." She is past eighty.

At the bottom of the ramp, the space expands into the large cavern of the lower floor, past what was formerly Leilani's Hawaiian Goods and Vi's Restaurant to the right (west). Leilani's has now moved to another market location nearby, and there is now a "psychedelic" shop at this spot. It is called Q-Ra3 Gallery Annex; the main gallery is in Pioneer Square. These changes are merely evidence that the market situation is not a static one.

Ahead are myriads of wooden columns and the busiest ceiling to be seen anywhere. All the vital parts of the building are exposed, with beams, purlins, subflooring, plumbing pipes and joints of all shapes and sizes, a complete fire-sprinkling system, electrical conduits, outlet boxes, switches, lamps both incandescent and fluorescent, and a few other functional (or formerly functional) contrivances and improvisations, including a considerable array of signs both old and new.

The POST OFFICE is one of the services maintained at the expense of the Pike Place Public Markets Corporation. Mr. Joe Desimone is said to have been the first postmaster, and there have been three postmistresses since that time. The present incumbent is Freda Judd, who has been there for sixteen years.

Well into the lower floor cavern, there is a choice of two general directions of movement. Forward and to the left (east) a stairway leads upward. To the right, in the distance, there is an upward ramp in view past the Post Office and the Dexter Gallery. Some shops here are Dr. Sussman Optometrist, Mr. Wright's Repair Shop, Market Coins, and now Leilani's Hawaiian Goods has moved to this location also.

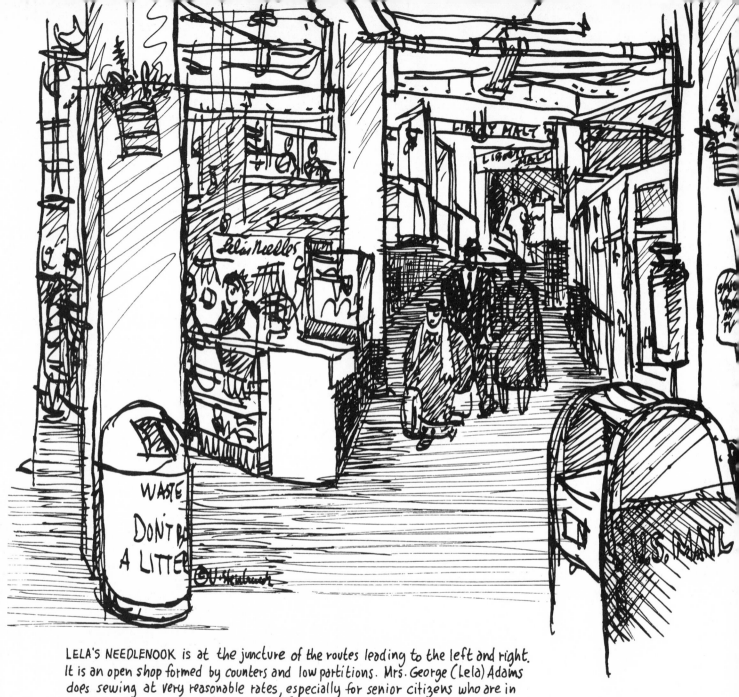

LELA'S NEEDLENOOK is at the juncture of the routes leading to the left and right. It is an open shop formed by counters and low partitions. Mrs. George (Lela) Adams does sewing at very reasonable rates, especially for senior citizens who are in need of buttons and mending. Three-fourths of her work is for pensioners.

DEXTER GALLERY is jointly operated by Marie Erickson and Herb Chilcote, who also runs the Dexter Ice Cream Parlor and Dexter Galleries on Dexter Avenue North. Marie is a tall, attractive blonde who wears a plentitude of bracelets, rings, brooches, earrings, and necklaces along with her cover-up smock. She also favors outlandish but handsome hair styles and ornaments appropriate to the occasion, such as the Fourth of July, St. Patrick's Day, or a visit from Governor Daniel J. Evans.

The LIBERTY MALT SHOP is a place to buy supplies for beer and wine making. Available are yeast, malt, crocks, siphons, and fermentation locks as well as helpful and conscientious advice.

The upholstery and furniture repair shop, BON TON UPHOLSTERING CO., is run by Mr. Sassanoff, who has been in the market since 1922. He left his native Russia on foot and made it out across Mongolia. His working hours are somewhat irregular, but he is most accommodating, and of course his prices are not excessive.

MARY'S CORNER and the BALCONY GIFT SHOP are both run by the same owner, so when one shop is not open, the other one probably is, or if a desired item is thought to be available in the other shop there will be some running back and forth. At first these shops offered inexpensive antiques, and now the merchandise has been expanded to include low-priced tourist gifts and souvenirs. Mary's Corner is in a space formerly unoccupied. The owners put up shelves and counters and wire screen partitions and called it a shop.

Up the back ramp to the west, past Bon Ton Upholstering Co. on one side and Balcony Gift Shop on the other, is a labyrinth of passageways, shops, and back entrances to serve the marketeer and beguile the wanderer. The plain door and window of the "market master" is located just down the ramp from the street level main arcade. From this passage there is access to the Italian Grocery, the Spice Shop, and the Dexter Ice Cream Parlor. This corridor is little used.

Herb Chilcote operates the DEXTER OLD-FASHIONED ICE CREAM PARLOR not only to serve fancy ice-cream dishes but also as a showplace for some of his antique lamps and furniture, and as a goodwill gesture to add color to the market. Superb hamburgers and superspecial ice-cream dishes can be enjoyed here in an atmosphere of marbletop tables and wire chairs, along with the magnificent panorama of Elliott Bay. Herb often works there himself and has taken a helpful interest in promoting the lower floor of the market, where he has set up several shops. The Friends of the Market always find Herb to be a friend indeed when help is needed.

"The market is a fragile kaleidoscope of merchants, mostly foreign born and fiercely independent. It provides an income for dozens of small businessmen and women of a breed embodying all the virtues, now almost gone, that we believe made America great. They survive because the atmosphere in which they live and work here is compatible with their way of life. They can survive in no other atmosphere.

"The market as it stands today is for all people. There is no discrimination....

"Can we not save a corner of our city as a place for human contact? Will this not help us to have a more unique and wonderful city?"
Quote from Elizabeth Tanner, Executive Secretary of Friends of the Market

The Flower Farmers' Ramp is little used at present although it is remembered for its bright luxuriant days when it was filled with cut flowers and potted plants. It is one of the most intriguing spaces in the market, with its stepped counters, decorative colonnade, and glorious view of the harbor. Now it is a convenient lounging area for market habitués and is used occasionally for public affairs by the Friends of the Market. There is ready access from the open concourse at Pike Place above. Flowers are now sold mainly in the arcade north of City Fish.

Back down in the lower floor cavern at Lela's Needlenook, the path to the left (east) leads past Dr. Sussman Optometrist to the incline of stairs up to DeLaurenti's Italian Grocery. Dr. David Sussman has been practicing his profession as an optometrist in the market for thirty years. Many of his clients are market area residents and old-age pensioners.

At the foot of the stairs are various byways with several antique stalls, the Market Print Shop, and an entrance to the Goodwill Store.

Alice Richter runs the one-woman MARKET PRINT SHOP, doing job printing on an old Chandler and Price press. Her shop is almost hidden down a narrow corridor between Janet's Corner and Grandma's Attic antique stalls.

Ruby Ruteloni's SPECIALTY SPICE SHOP is a world of aromas, with spices and herbs from all over the world for sale very inexpensively, as well as every kind of tea leaf and coffee bean available anywhere. Angelica, dill, rosemary, savory, sweet marjoram, oregano, tarragon, thyme, and other herbs and spices can be bought in bulk, freshly ground if desired. A small coffee counter serves freshly made coffee from freshly ground coffee beans.

DELAURENTI'S ITALIAN GROCERY is a gourmet's delight with its wealth of Mediterranean foods. Pete DeLaurenti and his wife Mamie-Marie are the proprietors and regular workers in this shop established by Angelina Mustello, Mrs. DeLaurenti's mother, in 1928. On the shelves and in the open sacks, boxes, and pails on the floor are countless varieties of pasta, cheeses, olives, beans, rice, olive oil, and imported foods. Regular customers are Italian, Greek, Jewish, French, and Slavic, but it is a favorite spot for all food adventurers and for tourists.

Ada Wilson barbers across from the Italian Grocery in ADA'S BALCONY BARBER SHOP. She was born in South Dakota in 1892 and came to Seattle in 1920. Before her husband died she used to help him on his fishing boat. She still bowls twice a week. Mrs. Wilson likes to work in the market because of her many friends, who stop by to chat with her and sometimes "to get clipped", as she says.

VAN'S SHOE REPAIR has been located here under other names for many years. The rumor that Block's Shoe Stores began here is probably not true—they did, however, begin somewhere in the market. The repairman and owner is I. Van Sickle, who worked for his predecessor and then bought the business from him after World War II. The assortment of used shoes for sale is a somewhat surrealistic display. The shop serves many of the area's old men, who may also drop in for just a visit or gossip. In recent years Mr. Van Sickle has reduced his space because of concern over the effect of urban renewal on the market, making room next door for Daffron's Antiques run by Frances and James Daffron,

Daylight pours in again as the stairway up to the big opening at Pike Street comes into view. A women's lavatory, the only one in the central business district maintained by the city, outside of public buildings, is available here.

At the top of the stairs the Flower Farmers' ramp is behind - now always with a number of the elderly men who live nearby visiting together there.

Down from the stairs to the right of the women's lavatory is a pair of doors opening onto another flight of wooden stairs leading to a wooden balcony walk serving the Goodwill Store and Jakk's Gallerie. Once this was part of a wooden pedestrian bridge over Railroad Avenue (now Alaskan Way) to the waterfront. One of the few parks in downtown Seattle, planted by Friends of Friends of the Market, is found in the converted street end.

The GOODWILL STORE is one of many salvage clothing and merchandise shops or "thrift" shops in the Pike Place area. These not only serve the needs of low-income shoppers, but also attract bargain seekers from all economic groups. From their stock it is possible to outfit a family or a home at the very minimum cost. These essential shops are a part of the supporting environment of the market and of its basic service to low-income people. For others, these used items make for interesting bargain hunting in the tradition of "flea markets" throughout the world.

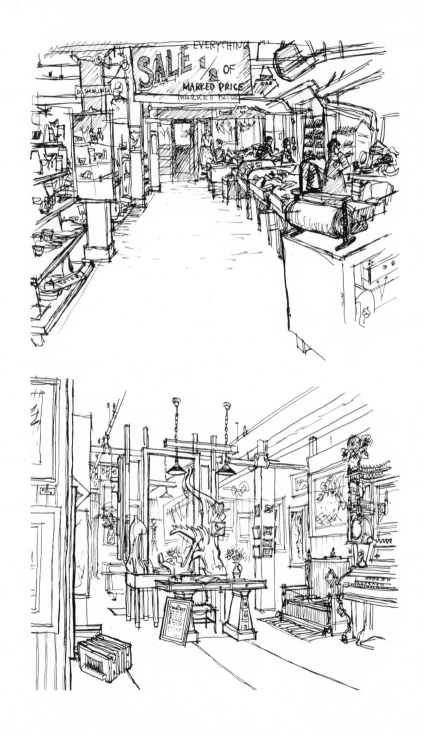

Colorful, bearded Jakk Corsaw manages his JAKK'S GALLERIE next to the Goodwill Store, with a varied collection of paintings, sculpture, and odd items of esthetic interest. He exhibits the work of several artists, including his own. Young Hans Nelsen, whose sketch of old shoes appears later in this book, was first handled commercially by Jakk. There is so much atmosphere in his individually styled gallery that it attracts throngs of tourists as one of the market showplaces. Depending on Jakk's convenience, it is open at irregular hours.

Here is the view out to Elliott Bay and Duwamish Head, with the Cliff House Hotel built in 1911 in the foreground. The LaSalle Hotel, adjacent to the left, was built in 1908. The other hotel within the public market building complex is the Leland Hotel of 1908, directly to the north and above this location. There are about one hundred residential units in these three hotels.

Seattle civic leader and architect Ibsen Nelsen says,
"The market has always been a vital and genuine place in both the highest and humblest sense. Its attraction for the poor — secondhand shops, rummage and horse meat places; for artists — color, movement and haphazard honesty; and for all kinds of people — a wonderful variety of vegetable stalls, meat counters, and specialty shops. If it needed renewal, it needed only modest structural repairs and simple maintenance. It needed assured continuity through public ownership; it needed efforts to encourage survival of farmlands and farmers near the city. And it needed to be left alone."

On a sunny afternoon, this open street-end park offers a welcome relief from the severities of downtown Seattle. Now destroyed through neglect, Richard Beyer's sculptured cedar wolf used to be a favorite of the children. Beautification and maintenance of this small green spot have been mainly the responsibility of the King County Grange, which provided the trees, shrubs, and ivy, and continues to give care and maintenance not yet assumed by the city.

Where Pike Street crosses First Avenue to the west, and turns north to
become Pike Place, there is another, less noticed, ramped street approach
from lower Post Street to the south. Post Street parallels First Avenue
south of this location. Down this ramp to Post Street are the
well-hidden Hideout Tavern, the Rice Bowl Café, and Boulton's Tavern, and
then a small dramatic theater, Stage One. There is also access to
Western Avenue by way of the little street-end park seen earlier, as
well as an entrance to the city-maintained men's lavatory.

This is one of the few locations in Seattle where building use over a street occurs. Possibly, before restrictive codes and ordinances were enacted, it was the obvious thing to do in this situation.

Where Post Street meets Pike Street it tunnels under some of the market buildings, to the advantage of both and to the architectural delight of those who discover it. The one-way approach from the south is reminiscent of the walled gates of a European town.

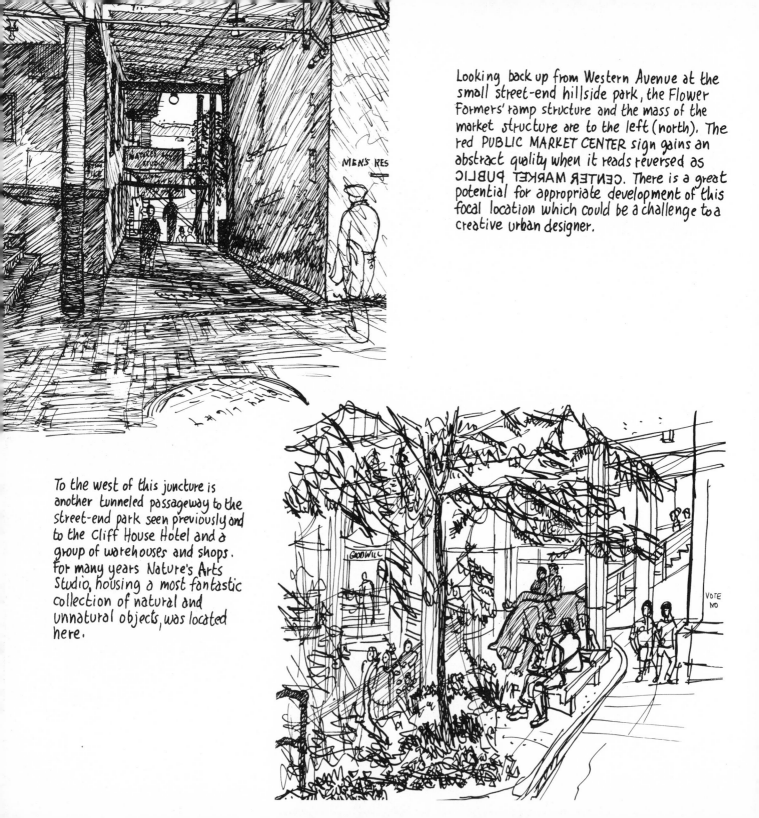

Looking back up from Western Avenue at the small street-end hillside park, the Flower Farmers' ramp structure and the mass of the market structure are to the left (north). The red PUBLIC MARKET CENTER sign gains an abstract quality when it reads reversed as ЯƎTИƎϽ TƎꓘЯAM ϽI⅃BUꟼ. There is a great potential for appropriate development of this focal location which could be a challenge to a creative urban designer.

MEN'S RES

To the west of this juncture is another tunneled passageway to the street-end park seen previously and to the Cliff House Hotel and a group of warehouses and shops. For many years Nature's Arts Studio, housing a most fantastic collection of natural and unnatural objects, was located here.

GOODWILL

VOTE NO

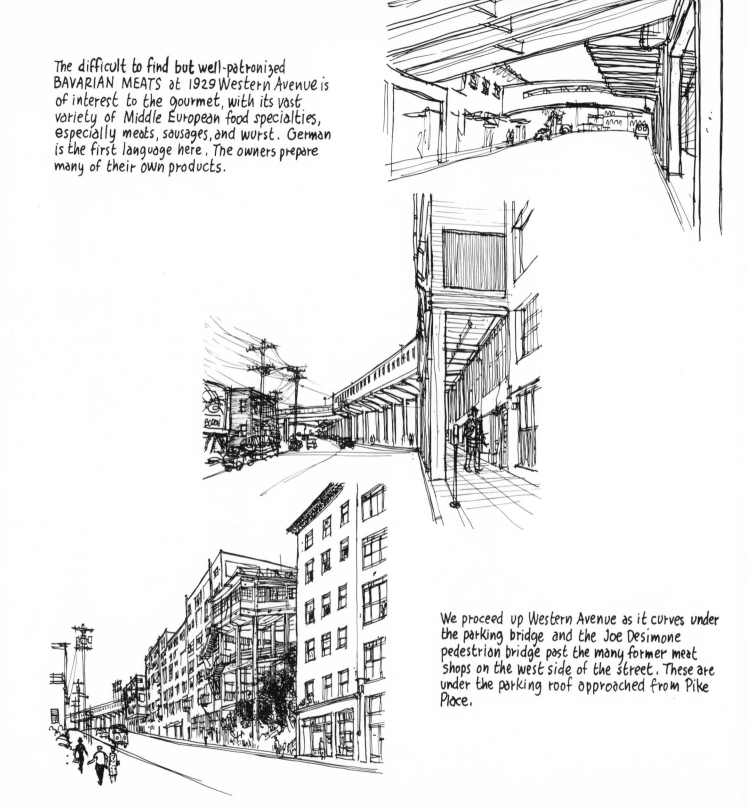

The difficult to find but well-patronized BAVARIAN MEATS at 1929 Western Avenue is of interest to the gourmet, with its vast variety of Middle European food specialties, especially meats, sausages, and wurst. German is the first language here. The owners prepare many of their own products.

We proceed up Western Avenue as it curves under the parking bridge and the Joe Desimone pedestrian bridge past the many former meat shops on the west side of the street. These are under the parking roof approached from Pike Place.

The mass of the main market building seen from the west along Western Avenue is a fascinating array of windows and simple architectural elements which form an impressive composition as well as being expressive of the interior spaces. Paint would do wonders in allowing the architectural interest of the structures to be appreciated. The lower floors are now used only for storage and maintenance, but there is a public doorway leading up to the main floor almost hidden in the center of this building.

One of the grandest downtown lookout places is at Western Avenue where it meets Pike Place and Virginia Street. It has been neglected by the city, and its possibilities for public enjoyment are ignored except by a few habitués and passing pedestrians.

Another approach to the public market is from this location moving south along Western Avenue into Pike Place, past the old concrete stalls and into the open market arcade. Key buildings in the central business district are visible from this vantage point along with the harbor view. The Joe Desimone bridge is seen arching over Western Avenue behind the market.

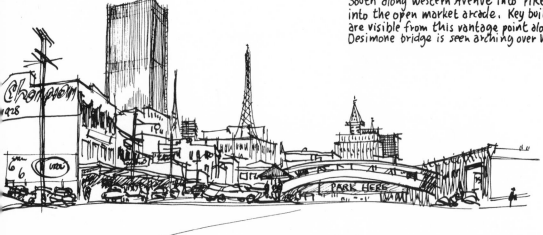

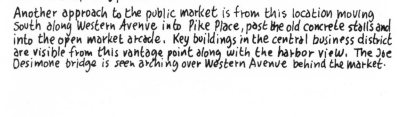

The old State Armory, a landmark since it was built before World War I, was knocked down in the spring of 1968 after a valiant and spirited effort had been made to save it for future restoration and development. Possibilities for colorful, realistic restoration of this characteristic armory structure into a series of shops were presented by Laurie Olin, a young architect, but the municipal wrecker's ball could not be stayed. Buildings like this (and there are very few) offer an irreplaceable tie with the past as well as adding variety and interest to new surroundings. Restoration is not at all impossible or difficult for sympathetic designers. Others can always find practical reasons for destruction.

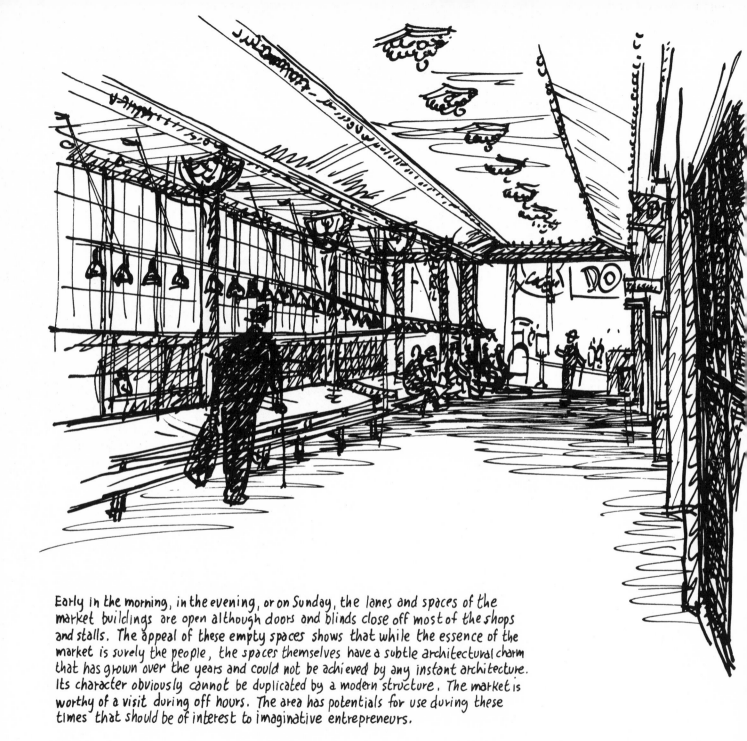

Early in the morning, in the evening, or on Sunday, the lanes and spaces of the market buildings are open although doors and blinds close off most of the shops and stalls. The appeal of these empty spaces shows that while the essence of the market is surely the people, the spaces themselves have a subtle architectural charm that has grown over the years and could not be achieved by any instant architecture. Its character obviously cannot be duplicated by a modern structure. The market is worthy of a visit during off hours. The area has potentials for use during these times that should be of interest to imaginative entrepreneurs.

Lowell's Café and the Athenian Tavern are open early in the morning to serve the market people. The rest of the shops are still closed off by heavy dark canvas blinds or wooden doors. The farmers' unoccupied stalls are left open.

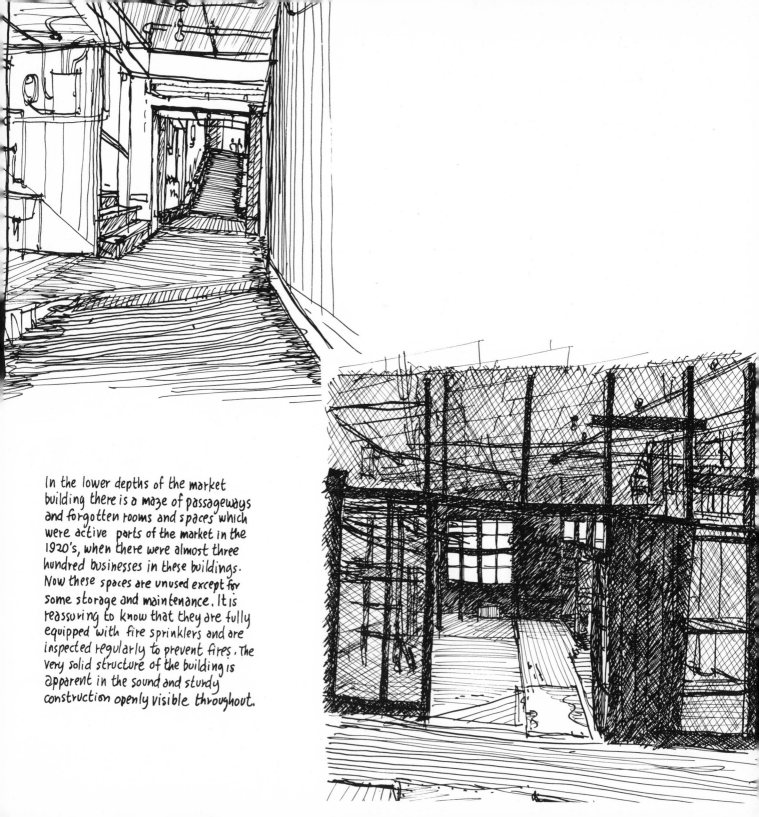

In the lower depths of the market building there is a maze of passageways and forgotten rooms and spaces which were active parts of the market in the 1920's, when there were almost three hundred businesses in these buildings. Now these spaces are unused except for some storage and maintenance. It is reassuring to know that they are fully equipped with fire sprinklers and are inspected regularly to prevent fires. The very solid structure of the building is apparent in the sound and sturdy construction openly visible throughout.

Robert D. Ashley, Seattle attorney and former co-chairman of Friends of the Market, writes,

"Thousands of Seattle citizens, joined by thousands of visitors from as far away as Hong Kong and London, are preparing to take a firm stand in defense of this major Seattle attraction if its future becomes threatened.

"Through the years, Seattleites of every national origin, race, religion, and economic status have been part of the market. They still are, and today eighteen nationalities and twenty-six spoken languages can be found within its bustling confines.

"People regard the market place fondly for a variety of reasons. It is the only place in Seattle where the farmer deals directly with the customer providing lots of noise and color along with bargains for low-income families as well as connoisseurs of good food. It is a center for art and students of art—Mark Tobey spent his early years there. The Pike Place Market is full of unexpected things, curious shops, great antique displays, unexpected cubbyholes and quaint passageways, even a live theater which presented a play by Shaw as its opening attraction recently.

"Concerned citizens know that too often in other cities, urban renewal programs have become programs of urban removal, and that isn't what they want to see happen in Pike Place. Urban renewal can help the market without destroying it, and its ability to rise above the occasion and truly renew the market rather than to remove it, would help vindicate the unfortunate reputation that urban renewal has earned in some cities by programs of indiscriminate destruction.

"The Pike Place Market cannot be torn down, rebuilt, and still be the market. It is a vital, healthy, stimulating oasis of genuine humanity in a world which has become increasingly insensitive to human values. The present buildings and their immediate surroundings are the market and should not be touched except for necessary painting, refurbishing, and structural repairs. This opinion is shared by all who know and care.

"True, the market is in a slight state of disarray—that is its personality—but it is no museum piece. It functions as vitally today as it did sixty years ago and throbs with today's, and hopefully tomorrow's, commerce. Business is good!"

These old photographs and postcards show where the market came from. In the beginning farmers brought their wagonloads of produce from Queen Anne Hill, Georgetown, South Park, Renton, and other nearby farm areas to sell directly to the public. In the fall of 1907, John and Frank Goodwin built a building for the farmers' use and for other food shops. The city was involved in controls but never in ownership. In 1927, there were more than four hundred farmers selling from the market. Extensive building and rebuilding took place around the time of World War I, and then again in the mid-twenties with architect Andrew Willatsen, A.I.A., doing the work for the Desimone family. He has done their work ever since that time and must be credited with maintaining the simple, anonymous, functional character of the structures. Other buildings are surviving symbols of past eras, and contribute to the overall character of the Pike Place cityscape. 1906 is thought to be the date of the above photograph looking north on Pike Place from Pike Street.

Postcard view (c. 1924) looking north on Pike Place from same viewpoint as 1906 photograph on opposite page.

Postcard view (c. 1912) looking east up Pike Street from Pike Place past First Avenue.

Julie Anderson, Seattle housewife and member of Friends of the Market, says,
"When I think of the market, I long to be a great poet or writer for it deserves no less. However, here are my feelings. For me the market is a happy combination of style and diversity. At a thrift shop, people are seeking warm winter coats which may cost only a dollar or two. Next door, in an antique shop, are those anxious to pay hundreds of dollars for Tiffany lamp shades. Ingredients for simple homemade soups are sold alongside exotic gourmet specialties. Farmers' hands are often roughened by hard work, while their manners are genteel and their intelligence bright.
"Being in the market makes me hungry and glad to be a housewife - eager to cook. It also speaks to my sense of values and asks for integrity because of the honesty and directness that exists there.
"While there, one cannot stay aloof or separated, one is involved with life as a human fact."

The market has always attracted and challenged artists because of its concentration and variety of people, places, things, and activities not to be found elsewhere in the Northwest. The constantly changing human and environmental circumstances contrast greatly with the usual compartmented contemporary shopping center situation, making the market a place of tremendous emotional, dramatic, and esthetic appeal. It is the least superficial of places wherein to penetrate the spirit of the people.
The easy, accepted, free flow of exchange between buyers and sellers without reference to economic status, color, or creed has established a precedent for living that needs to be nurtured to continue and to grow.
Major alteration or dislocation of this environment will inevitably destroy the combination of people and the particular diversified daily market life built up over sixty years. As Fred Bassetti says, "It needs the hammer and paint brush, not the black ball of destruction."
The sketch by Mark Tobey represents the work of an established artist who is devoted to the market and what its survival means for our city and our society.

Young Hans Nelsen's sketch of the old shoes in the Goodwill Store is one of many that he has made in the market and in Seattle. Hans was born in 1952 and attends Garfield High School. His sketch is included for its interest and as a symbol of hope for the mutual future of the market and artists together.

SAVE
THE
MARKET

Acknowledgments

Thanks are gratefully tendered to the following: the Friends of the Market organization and individuals for generous help of all kinds whenever needed and for encouragement and sponsorship; the people of the market who gave information and who made it pleasant for me to work in the market; Elizabeth Tanner for endless help and for her quote; Julie Anderson for gathering much of the information about the market people and for her quote; my wife, Marjorie, for sincere interest and helpful criticism and for typing the manuscript; Robert Ashley for friendly insistence that I do this book and for his quote; Astra Zarina-Haner for touching up some of my sketches while I was in London; Ken Wagner for taking photographs for me and for the use of others; Gordon Varey for touching up some of my lettering; Mark Tobey for use of his sketch and for his quote; Hans Nelsen for use of his sketch; Fred Bassetti and Ibsen Nelsen for their quotes; Richard Desimone for information about the history of the market and for loaning the old photograph of his father; the Northwest Collection of the University of Washington Library and its curator, Robert C. Monroe, for use of the two old postcards; Arthur B. Andersen and Tom Gay for the use of plans, diagrams, and photographs; my son, Peter, for sketching in the market with me; many others who have aided in countless ways; and to the Seattle office of Urban Renewal for making it necessary to do this book as an effort to help save the market and its essential environs.

Almost all of the sketches were made on location with a Mont Blanc fountain pen on Strathmore high surface paper. The hand lettering was done with a Rapidograph pen.

It will be found that people, businesses, and buildings have changed as time goes by, since the market is not static, but is in a constant state of evolution. It is hoped that the changes will be sympathetic to the purpose and character of the market which have inspired this sketchbook.

August, 1968
London, England

VICTOR STEINBRUECK, F.A.I.A.